Other Helen Exley giftbooks with cartoons by Roland Fiddy:
The Victim's Guide to Middle Age   The Fight Against Gravity
The Fanatic's Guide to Sex   A Special Gift for Big Tum
A Special Gift for Baldy   The Fanatic's Guide to Cats
The wrinklies guide to staying Young at Heart

Published simultaneously in 1998 by Exley Publications Ltd in Great Britain, and
Exley Publications LLC in the USA.
Text copyright © Stuart and Linda Macfarlane 1998.
Cartoons copyright © Roland Fiddy 1998.

12   11

Written by Stuart and Linda Macfarlane.
Cartoons by Roland Fiddy.
Edited by Helen Exley.

ISBN 1-86187-094-9

A copy of the CIP data is available from the British Library on request.

Printed in China.

Exley Publications Ltd, 16 Chalk Hill, Watford, Herts WD19 4BG, UK.
Exley Publications LLC, 232 Madison Avenue, Suite 1409, NY 10016, USA.
www.helenexleygiftbooks.com

THE LITTLE BOOK OF

STRESS

BY STUART & LINDA MACFARLANE
CARTOONS BY ROLAND FIDDY

A HELEN EXLEY GIFTBOOK

EXLEY
NEW YORK • WATFORD, UK

PANIC!
Surround your bed with alarm clocks
and start the day
with a crash, bang, wallop.

MAKE A HIT LIST

Begin each day
by making a list of all the things
you have to do.
Resolve not to rest until
every task is complete.

START THE WEEK WITH DREAD

Wake up every morning with that Monday Morning feeling. The thought of a full week ahead will prime your heart for attack.

GROAN

CONFUSE US SAYS:
"Avoid Monday morning blues – work
night shifts."
"Monday morning blues can easily
be avoided by working
seven days a week."

TICK...TICK.

TICK...TICK...

TORMENT OF TIME
Set your wristwatch
to beep every fifteen minutes
and constantly review your progress
to ensure your time is purposely filled.
Become a time-control fanatic.
Count every second
and make every second count.

SET HIGH EXPECTATIONS
Strive for perfection
in everything you do.
Total failure
will result from even the smallest
imperfection.

CONFUSE US SAYS:
"Only reach for the stars
if you are on the payroll of NASA."

SURROUND YOURSELF WITH CRITICS
Surround yourself with highly ambitious,
aggressive and dominant people
who will constantly criticize you.
Accept their criticism as an insight
into your weaknesses and failings.

idiot.

SPEND UP TO THE LIMIT
Having money in the bank is pointless.
It is of no use to you when you are dead.
Always be heavily in debt.
Aim to spend 20% more than you earn
as this will encourage you to work hard
for a large pay rise.

GO FOR JET LAG
"Be a Frequent Flier –
stress out in two time zones
at once."

PLAY TO WIN

Use sport to hone
your competitive edge.
Play to win at all costs
as losing is proof of failure.
Remember:
It's not the taking part
it's the winning
that counts.

SHOP AT PEAK TIMES
Supermarkets can provide a useful boost
to your stress level
if you shop at peak times.
Choose a shopping cart with wobbly wheels
and make sudden changes of direction.
Pay at the less-than-ten-items till
and argue that you do not have time
to count items.

CONFUSE US SAYS:
"Fast foods
take sixty seconds to cook
and sixty minutes
to buy."

RUSH!

BLOW YOUR MIND
Use your quadraphonic sound system
to simultaneously play heavy rock
and classical music
at high volume.
This clash of styles
will send adrenalin pulsing
through your veins
and set your heart pounding.

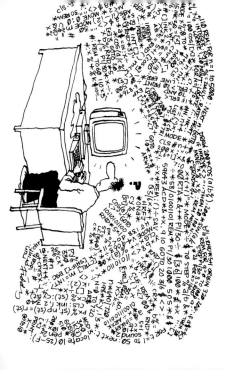

HAVE AN ALL NIGHT STRESS SESSION

Leave all your revision
to the night before exams.
Resits will allow you to
have such sessions on a regular basis.

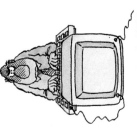

MEGABYTE

Buy a computer.

(Minimum spec: 486 Mhz 140 BHP
512KB cache 32MB SDRAM PAS SCSI
ABS x16CD.)

CONFUSE US SAYS:

"Computers can solve problems
you previously did not have."

BE JUST IN TIME

Valuable time
can be saved
by arriving at the
airport just as,
"Will Mr and Mrs Strane
please make their way
to terminal two
as the plane is about to take off,"
is announced for the final time.

REMEMBER YOUR FAILURES

Frequently reflect on past failures
and weaknesses.

Those many occasions of incompetence.
Use these thoughts as motivation
to achieve your desired goals —
but keep asking yourself
whether you have really overcome
those inadequacies.

CONFUSE US SAYS:
"Experience
is the ability to recognize
a mistake
when you make it again."

Take a "No smiles today" resolution.

FIGHT TO WIN

Keep your mind agile and under pressure
by constantly seeking arguments.
Set basic ground rules:

a) You must win at all costs even when
in the wrong.

b) You must get your opponent to
admit fault.

c) There is never any justification
for compromise.

CONFUSE US SAYS:
"For every winner there is a loser
planning the next battle."
"The person who wins all arguments
celebrates alone."

HOUT!

BATTLE PLAN

With your partner make a list of
each other's bad habits and little irritations.
Battle together to overcome these.
Pin a weekly score-chart on the wall and see
which of you is making greater progress.

GET MARRIED

GO FOR CAFFEINE

Drink as much tea and coffee as possible.
The caffeine will help you stay awake
and get another couple of hours
out of each day.

SUN, SEA AND STRESS

Avoid holidays whenever possible.
When they are unavoidable
make sure you tell everyone at the office
how to contact you in a crisis.
Pack your computer and modem.
This way your frantic lifestyle
can continue as normal.

FRENZY OF CHANGE
Move house. Change job. Move house
and change job. Change your partner.
Move house, change your job
and your partner.
If it can change, change it frequently.

FORGET WHAT PEACE IS
Have children.

CONFUSE US SAYS:
"Children are the answer to all your problems
and the problem to all your answers."

DANGER! DO-IT-YOURSELF

Shock the family
with your home maintenance skills
by undertaking every task yourself.
While toiling away keep your nerves on edge
with the thought that:

- 78% of house fires are caused
  by faulty wiring
- 93% of serious personal injuries
  occur while carrying out
  home maintenance
- 71% of gas explosions
  are a direct result
  of grossly incompetent,
  amateur workmanship.

CONFUSE US SAYS:
"Disasters
don't come with instruction manuals."
"Accidents
don't happen by accident —
you need to work at them."

LOSE HOPE
Increase the chance of your lottery numbers being chosen.
Lose your lottery ticket half an hour before the draw.

CONFUSE US SAYS:
"6, 7, 18, 29, 32, 42 –
guaranteed to win once in the next
657,862,106 years."

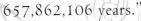

RACE AGAINST TIME
Life is short.
You could die at any time.
Remind yourself of this by regularly
attending funerals.
There is no need to stay for the whole service,
this would be wasting time.
Arrange for your phone to ring
shortly after the service begins
giving you an excuse to leave.

FORGET PLANNING

Planning takes up a lot of time and resources.
Always impress the boss
by vastly underestimating cost and time.
Try to find another job
before the inevitable disaster occurs.

CONFUSE US SAYS:
"Plan carefully for the future
and you will never run out of
cabbage."

FASHION VICTIM

Tight shoes are a source of irritation.
They should be worn
as a constant reminder
that you cannot slacken in your resolve
to achieve success at all costs.

BE AN IDIOT, TAKE ALL THE KIDS!
On a sunny summers day
cram the car full of your kids and their friends
and take them for a trip to the beach.
During the long, hot drive
keep their excitement aroused by
playing with beach balls
and loudly singing "1000 Green Bottles".

CRAZY

OVER COMMIT YOURSELF

Determine your goals in life
and allocate time appropriately
to achieve these.
Each week:
work 104 hours,
family and personal 36 hours,
sleep 28 hours.
If urgent family needs demand extra time
it should not be taken from those hours
allocated to work.

CONFUSE US SAYS:
"Time is infinite
but each week is always ten hours short."

SELL YOUR SOUL
Make full use of your spare time.
If you already have a second job
take on a third.

CONFUSE US SAYS:
"Wealth and happiness
are the same side
of a different coin."

R.RRING!

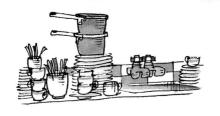

DO IT ALL
Remember
all around you
suffer from gross incompetence.
You must do
even the most menial task yourself.

DIET FAILURE

Fit a full-size mirror in your bedroom.
Daily study how overweight and unfit
you have become and repeat five times
"I'm a fat, lazy slob."
Resolve to exercise and diet until you achieve
the body of a supermodel.

CONFUSE US SAYS:

"The mirror image of sweet is bitter."

GO TO AN UGLY, NOISY PLACE

Find a busy spot in the heart of the city
and go there often. Breathe in the atmosphere.
Watch the stress-lines on the anonymous people
rushing past. Let the tension
penetrate your heart.

CONFUSE US SAYS:
"Towns make strangers,
cities make strangers stranger."

NIGHT FRIGHT
Arrange some nights home alone
to watch really scary movies.
Later as you lie awake in bed
in the eerie darkness
imagine how easily something awful
could happen to you.

ORGANIZED CHAOS

The hours spent looking for
important documents are not wasted.
Consider it a part of your security system.
After all, if you can't find them
neither can a thief.

CONFUSE US SAYS:

"Chaos is simply your documents
neatly organized in random order."
"If you run out of space on the floor
consider using the filing cabinet."

BE UNPREPARED

Preparing for meetings and presentations
is time consuming and reduces spontaneity.
Rely on your natural ability to remember
huge amounts of detail and to present it
in a flashy, confident manner.

CONFUSE US SAYS:
"If 'a picture paints a thousand words'
a few good bar graphs
could leave you speechless."

ORGANIZE YOUR TEENAGERS
Round up your teenagers
at eight o'clock every Saturday night
and insist on sharing family quality time.
Thrash out all family disputes before going
on to play charades and happy families.

DO YOUR DUTY
Visit your relatives!!!

WATCH TIME TAKE ITS TOLL
A morning glance into the bathroom mirror
is a good reminder that you have a finite time
to live. Watch for the warning signs of receding h
sagging tummy and stress-lines appearing –
these mark the passing of time.

CONFUSE US SAYS:
"The only alternative
to old age is best avoided."
"The only guarantee in life
is that you will never benefit from
your life insurance policy."

DEAR!

ENDLESS WORRY

The things you are worrying about
tend not to happen.
Therefore there must be many more serious
things that you should be worrying about.
Strive to find out what these are
to give greater purpose to your efforts
and enhance your feelings of panic.

CONFUSE US SAYS:
"Don't seek the answer
until you have found the problem."

SUFFER IN SILENCE
Gain maximum stress
from a problem
by dealing with it entirely on your own.
Confiding in others
reduces the pressure.

THE END
There is no end –
your worries go on forever.